Thank you for your purchase. May every prayer in this book help you strengthen your prayer life.

VISIONARY AUTHOR
EVANGELIST O'KEIYA DINNALL

Prayers of a Mother's Heart

DEDICATION

This book is dedicated to all the moms around the world... just a reminder that the Lord hears the prayers of a mother's heart ♥

TABLE OF CONTENTS

*Evangelist
O'Keiya
Dinnall*

PRAYERS FROM OKEIYA'S HEART

A PRAYER FOR MY DAUGHTER

Dear God,

I come before You with a mother's heart, lifting my daughter to You. You know the plans You have for her, plans to prosper her and give her hope and a future. I pray that You guide her steps and lead her to the man You have chosen for her, a man who will love, honor, and cherish her as You intended.

Grant her wisdom and discernment in her relationships. Help her to recognize the qualities of a Godly husband and to seek a partner who shares her faith and values. May she be patient and trust in Your timing, knowing that Your plans are perfect, and Your love is unfailing.

Protect her heart from disappointment and guide her away from relationships that are not in alignment with Your will. Surround her with supportive friends and family who will encourage her and uplift her during this journey. Let her feel Your presence and peace as she waits for Your divine plan to unfold.

Bless the man You have chosen for her, preparing his heart and mind to be a loving and faithful husband. May he be a man of integrity, kindness, and strength, who will walk beside her in faith and love. Together, may they build a home that honors You and reflects Your love to the world.

Thank You, Lord, for Your guidance and provision. I trust in Your perfect plan for my daughter and pray that she finds the husband You have destined for her. In Jesus' name, I pray, amen.

A PRAYER FOR MY SON FOR GOD'S FAVOR

Heavenly Father,

I come before You today, lifting my son in prayer. Lord, I ask for Your divine wisdom, knowledge, and guidance to be upon him. You are the source of all wisdom and understanding, and I pray that You will fill his heart and mind with Your truth.

Grant him a hunger and thirst for righteousness, O Lord. May he seek after Your ways and long to know You more deeply. As it is written in Matthew 5:6, "Blessed are those who hunger and thirst for righteousness, for they shall be filled." I pray that my son will be blessed with a desire to live a life that is pleasing to You.

Father, I ask that You surround him with Your favor. Let him find favor in Your sight and in the sight of others. As it is written in Luke 2:52, "And Jesus increased in wisdom and stature, and in favor with God and man." May my son grow in wisdom and stature, and may he walk in Your favor all the days of his life.

Guide his steps, Lord, and lead him on the path of righteousness. Show him the way he should go and help him to make wise decisions. May Your Word be a lamp to his feet and a light to his path, as it is written in Psalm 119:105. Illuminate his way, Lord, and let him walk in Your truth.

Lord, I pray for his protection. Keep him safe from harm and guard his heart and mind. Surround him with Your angels and let no weapon formed against him prosper. May he find refuge in You and trust in Your unfailing love.

A PRAYER FOR MY SON FOR GOD'S FAVOR CONTINUED...

I also pray for his relationships, Father. May he be surrounded by Godly friends who will encourage him and build him up. Let him be a light to those around him and may his life be a testimony of Your goodness and grace.

Lord, I ask for Your blessings upon his studies and endeavors. Grant him the knowledge and understanding he needs to excel in his pursuits. May he use the gifts and talents You have given him to serve You and others faithfully.

Father, I entrust my son to You, knowing that You have a wonderful plan for his life. Help him to trust in You and seek Your will in all things. May he grow in faith and love, and may his life bring glory to Your name.

Thank You, Lord, for hearing my prayer. I trust in Your promises and believe that You will guide my son in wisdom, knowledge, and righteousness. I pray all these things in the mighty name of Jesus, amen.

Love,
Mom
Okeiya Dinnall

A PRAYER FOR MY FAMILY

Dear Heavenly Father,

You have provided for me and my family, Lord you are so good to us, and I praise your name because you are Jehovah Jireh, you are our provider. Lord in your word you say that you shall supply all our needs according to your riches and glory in heaven and Lord, I thank you for providing over and over again. That you are always making a way out of no way you are always showing up for us, you are always on time. Lord you are so good to us and I am just so amazed by you. You continue to keep your hand of protection upon my family and for that I just tell you thank you Lord for protecting us. I thank you God that we can call upon your name and you are right there. For in your word you said that you would never leave us or forsake us, father, I thank you for being right there for my family. Lord, I thank you how you cover my children and how you cover my grandchildren, Lord, I thank you Lord God for breathing the breath of life upon them.

Father God you are so merciful that you give us new grace and mercy every day and I'm so thankful that surely goodness and mercy follows me and my family all the days of our life and that we shall dwell in the House of the Lord. Lord I thank you God for on the days that we feel weak you give us strength on the days when we are weary you are the wind beneath our wings so father God I praise your name I declare victory over my family. I know that we are more than a conqueror because you are with us every step of the way.

A PRAYER FOR MY FAMILY CONTINUED...

I know that we are more than conquerors because you are with us every step of the way. Father God I pray Deuteronomy 28 that we are blessed in the city blessed in the field blessed going in blessed going out that the blessings will continue to flow throughout my family from generation to generation. Now Lord I will forever praise your name I will remind my family daily of all the prayers that have been answered that I will continue to look to the hills which cometh my help and all my help coming from the Lord who made heaven and earth. Father God in the days to come I just ask that you will continue to give us a hunger and thirst after righteousness. Lord God continue to order my families steps. I declare victory over my family in Jesus' name, amen.

"Blessed shalt thou be in the city, and blessed in the field. shall be the fruit of thy body, and the fruit of thy ground, and the fruit of thy cattle, the increase of thy kine, and the flocks of thy sheep. thy basket and thy store. when thou comest in, and blessed when thou goest out." **-Deuteronomy 28:3-6 KJV**

Deuteronomy 8:18 (NIV)

"But remember the Lord your God, for it is he who gives you the ability to produce wealth, and so confirms his covenant, which he swore to your ancestors, as it is today."

Dear Heavenly Father,

I come before You with a heart full of gratitude for the blessings You have bestowed upon my family. I thank You for the promise in Deuteronomy 8:18, which reminds us that it is You who gives us the power to get wealth. I pray that You bless my children with wisdom, strength, and the ability to recognize and seize the opportunities You place before them.

Lord, I ask that You guide them in their endeavors and protect them from harm. Help them to walk in Your ways and to always remember that their success comes from You. May they remain humble and grateful for Your provision, and may their lives be a testament to Your goodness and faithfulness.

Father, I trust in Your word and believe that You will lead them to prosperity and fulfillment according to Your divine plan. Surround them with Your love and grace and let them feel Your presence in every step they take. In Jesus' name, amen.

For it is written, He shall give his angels charge over thee, to keep thee: **(KJV Luke :10)**

Dear Lord,

I pray today for my children and grandchildren, Lord your word says that you will give your angels charge over them. Lord let protection angels be around them every day. Please protect them from hurt, harm and dangers seen and unseen. Lord be with them all day long. Let them get back home daily safe and sound. Protect them from all that is evil. Let them have a good day. Guide their footsteps that stay away from harm. Lord let your hand be upon them. Father, I ask that you put a wall of protection all around them. Father, I stand on your word that no weapon form against them shall prosper. Lord fight every battle for them. I speak victory over their day. Lord let them have God encounters and see your glory upon there life.

Lord, I thank you for keeping my children and grandchildren. Amen

"All your children shall be taught by the LORD,
And great shall be the peace of your children."
(Isaiah 54:13)

Dear Lord,

Hear my cry, a cry from a mother's heart. Lord, I pray that my children are taught by You. Lord, that You will give them wisdom from heaven. Let them make the right decisions. Lord, speak to their heart, mind, and spirit. Father, open their eyes so that they can see you. Lord, pour out your love on my children, fill them up until they overflow. Oh God, that my children will do great and mighty things in this world. Give them a hunger and thirst for you, God. I speak victory over my children, touch them in every area of their lives. You are Lord Almighty, be the wind beneath their wings when they are weak. God, let my children soar like eagles, let them fly high above the storms of life. Lord, you watch over your word to perform it. I speak great things over my children. Lord, let the favor of God be upon their life. As you were with Moses, I ask that you be with my children. May they be strong and courageous. Grant them the strength to face challenges and the grace to be kind and compassionate. Lord, give them the grace to run their race for you. Father, I pray in the name of Jesus, I count it all done, amen.

For we are God's masterpiece. He has created us anew in Christ Jesus, so we can do the good things he planned for us long ago.
(Ephesians 2:10 NIV)

Dear Lord,

God, you have graced every child of God with a miraculous gift on the inside of them. These gifts are beyond his or her own natural ability. God, I ask that you would activate and stir up the gifts and talents on the inside of my children and grandchildren. Lord, let them use their gifts and talents with wisdom. That they will rise up and do great and mighty things in this earth. Father let my children and grandchildren have whitey and creative ideas. Lord bless the work of their hands. Oh Lord, let the power of the holy spirit flow through them. God, you created them to do a great work in this earth. Father, you said that my children and grandchildren are your masterpiece, your handiwork that you made to do a great work. May they use their talents to glorify You and serve others. Guide them in discovering their passions and give them the courage to pursue their dreams. Fill them with confidence and joy as they grow in their gifts. Father, I thank you and I bless your Holy name, amen.

"For we are God's masterpiece. He has created us anew in Christ Jesus, so we can do the good things he planned for us long ago."
(Ephesians 2:10 NIV)

Dear Lord,

Hear my cry, a cry from a mother's heart. Lord, I pray that my children are taught by You. Lord, that You will give them wisdom from heaven. Let them make the right decisions. Lord, speak to their heart, mind, and spirit. Father, open their eyes so that they can see you. Lord, pour out your love on my children, fill them up until they overflow. Oh God, that my children will do great and mighty things in this world. Give them a hunger and thirst for you, God. I speak victory over my children, touch them in every area of their lives. You are Lord Almighty, be the wind beneath their wings when they are weak. God, let my children soar like eagles, let them fly high above the storms of life. Lord, you watch over your word to perform it. I speak great things over my children. Lord, let the favor of God be upon their life. As you were with Moses, I ask that you be with my children. May they be strong and courageous. Grant them the strength to face challenges and the grace to be kind and compassionate. Lord, give them the grace to run their race for you. Father, I pray in the name of Jesus, I count it all done, amen.

LET'S PRAY...

Heavenly Father,
I thank You for being the shepherd of my children, guiding them through life's journey. Just as You lead us beside still waters, I pray that You grant them peace and tranquility in their hearts. May they always feel Your presence and know that You are with them, providing comfort and strength.

Lord,
As my children walk through the valleys of life, I ask that You protect them from harm and fear. Your rod and staff are their comfort, and I trust in Your divine protection. Help them to face challenges with courage and faith, knowing that You are their refuge and fortress.

Gracious God,
Prepare a table before them, even in the presence of their adversaries. Bless them with Your abundance and anoint their heads with oil, so their cups overflow with Your goodness and mercy. May they experience Your blessings in every aspect of their lives, and may Your love surround them always.

Loving Father,
I pray that Your goodness and mercy follow my children all the days of their lives. Let them dwell in Your house forever, finding joy and fulfillment in Your presence. Guide them on the path of righteousness, and may they grow in faith, wisdom, and love, amen.

Use the space below to write a prayer for your children.

O'KEIYA DINNALL

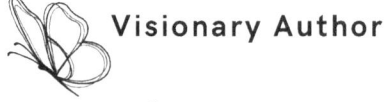

Visionary Author

Okeiya Dinnall is a devoted mother of two and a proud grandmother of three. A native of Brunswick County, she has been happily married for 29 years. Okeiya serves as the Assistant Director at a recovery center for women, where she passionately supports and empowers those on their journey to healing.

In her free time, Okeiya loves dancing in the rain with her grandchildren, creating joyful memories that last a lifetime. Her faith in God is unwavering, and she firmly believes in the power of prayer, holding onto the promise that "the prayers of the righteous availeth much." Okeiya is also the founder of With My Sister Inc. Outreach and released her first devotional book, *Built for the Battle*, in September 2024.

Ashley Kidwell

PRAYERS FROM ASHLEY'S HEART

I AM COMPASSIONATE AND DETERMINED

I am compassionate and determined.

I wonder sometimes why so many people have to hurt.

I hear doves singing. I see the dust on the baseboards.

I want to find recovery and stay sober.

I am compassionate and determined.

I pretend that I am perfect and that life is always great.

I feel overwhelmed and anxious.

I touch the Earth.

I worry that my children will be hurt and repeat my sins.

I cry when my children struggle.

I am compassionate and determined.

I understand that I am a child of God and he forgives me.

I say that if He can forgive me, I can forgive me.

I worry that my children will find unforgiveness toward me.

I cry when I realize I am not perfect.

I AM compassionate and determined.

I understand that no one is perfect - we just do our best.

I say that I am better today than I was yesterday.

I dream about success and my children's future.

I try to plan for their success.

I hope I lead them by example and remain the superhero in their story.

I am compassionate and determined.

I am a mother recovering from the illness of addiction. I was a broken shell of a soul, desperately seeking help in all the wrong places. In my anger and emptiness, I had turned away from God and lived a life of sin, trying to fill empty voids with drugs and sex, always teetering on the edge of death. God never turned away from me though and in my darkest place, he blessed me with a beautiful promise, the promise to become a mother. I was sick and getting ready to do the last of my drugs and as I was preparing for the high, I spilled the powder and had an inability to save any of it. I sat on a public bathroom floor, crying and pathetic, begging God for a change. The next day I learned that I was pregnant and that sweet child, forming in my womb, was the help God knew I desperately needed. From that moment on, I chose life so that my children may live, and I remain sober, faithful, and blessed as a mother of two little girls. For my daughters, this I pray:

"Heavenly Father, I thank you every day for the second chance in life you have trusted me to have. I thank you for the intervention and the opportunity to live the life I did so that I may be beneficial to your kingdom and serve you in ways I never knew was possible. Lord, I ask that you provide my children with the blessings and curses of life so that they may love you, hear your voice, and hold fast unto you. I beg that they may never encounter a burden too heavy to bear so that they never experience the same emptiness that I felt, but I ask that you strengthen me in my faith so that I may guide them and love them the way you loved your son and continue to love your children. Thank you, God, for trusting me with these beautiful souls, an assignment I will cherish for the remainder of my life on Earth. In Jesus' name, amen".

"This day I call the heavens and the earth as witnesses against you that I have set before you life and death, blessings and curses. Now choose life, so that you and your children may live."
-Deuteronomy 30:19 NIV

As children of God, we do not know when the end of days will be here. As a mother of children, it is not my calling to deliver undue anxiety on my children and raise them in fear and unknowingness of the future. For as Christians, this day should not scare us but rather be a silent thought of rejoice in the back of our minds. If we let the anxieties of the unknown dictate our everyday living, we might find ourselves short tempered, impatient, and unloving. We should not allow ourselves to sleep, blind to the needs of others and complacent just skating by. We should be awake and sober, belonging to the day and clothing ourselves in the armor of God – faith and salvation will protect us daily. Raising two little girls causes me to be intentional with the way I teach them to interact with others. Reminding them daily that we do not hurt other people physically or with our words, instead teaching them to be patient with all and discourage those who would rather pay back wrong for wrong. And with these thoughts I pray:

"Heavenly Father, as I approach my interactions with people throughout the world, I ask that you give me strength and patience so that I may lead my children by example. Cure me from the sin of gossip and mean-spirited comments so that the words that escape my mouth radiate love, patience, and a compassion that is lacking in this world. Help me to find the good in every person and to love them as you love us, meeting us where we are, free from judgment. As my daughters encounter trials through people, please give them the courage to not match wrong for wrong and to love endlessly the person who might sin against them. As they navigate life and encounter different situations, I ask that you give them the courage to stand up for the weak, encourage the disheartened, and warn those who are idle and disruptive. For it is through the armor of God they place on their hearts every day that they will trust and have faith that you are with them, and you will protect them. In Jesus' name I pray, amen".

And we urge you, brothers and sisters, warn those who are idle and disruptive, encourage the disheartened, help the weak, be patient with everyone. Make sure that nobody pays back wrong for wrong, but always strive to do what is good for each other and for everyone else. **-1 Thessalonians 5:14 NIV**

To Richard, a sweet and resilient baby:

Your mother was a faithful believer in Jesus Christ. A powerful woman, destined for great things, who was called home after her purpose was fulfilled. In an act of motherly selflessness, she held on just long enough to make sure your testimony of resilience could begin. A fighter like your mother, your story will one day have the power to touch thousands. A glorious testament to the power of love, faith, and Jesus Christ.

Her prayer for you, her precious child, was that you never know the generational curses that haunted her thoughts. She prayed that you only know love and acceptance in abundance, the same love and acceptance she was given from her family. She asked that God touch your mind, body, and soul and show you limitless mercy and grace as you live your life in honor of Him.

"Heavenly Father, I thank you for the impossible that produced a miracle. I pray that you use this child as a vessel for you and an unwavering show of your divine power. God, I ask that you show him the love that his mother had for him and bring comfort to his grieving spirit - a grief a child should not have to bear. But from his grief, Father God, I beg for him to find the words, the power, and the wisdom to find the other brokenhearted and restore their faith in you. Please use this child's story so that this death might not be in vain, and this child can continue to save those around him, just as his mother would have him do. I ask please that you keep him close to you, protect him, and encourage him every day. In Jesus name I pray, amen".

"For I wrote you out of great distress and anguish of heart and with many tears, not to grieve you but to let you know the depth of my love for you."
-2 Corinthians 2:4 NIV

Families are missing faith. We spend our days plugged into our smart phones, too ingrained to even acknowledge our children, our spouse, or our friends. Endless scrolling, brain rotting entertainment, and another opportunity for the enemy to reach us in ways so subtle.

This constant disconnection is a gateway to destruction. Yet we crave answered prayers from the one we call Father to rectify destruction in our lives. Imagine our unanswered prayers are just the prayers falling on a distracted parent scrolling social media. For my children I admit I can and should do better. I would never intentionally embitter my child.

When we give our lives to God, we allow our families to have a sense of togetherness. If we prioritized His word the way we prioritize our entertainment, our children would flourish, our marriages would reach new heights, and our relationships would improve.

"Heavenly Father, I come to you today with a need to be forgiven. Please forgive me Lord for disregarding my children today. Please forgive me for prioritizing my phone over the word of God. Please help me to see that if I prioritize your word, I can share this information with my family God. Your word tells us that a family founded in faith will reap a profound sense of togetherness. I want that togetherness; I need the togetherness. God, I thank you for not ignoring my prayers, for encouraging my growth and for not discouraging my calling to serve you. I pray that my children know a mother who serves them the same way: answered requests and encouraged growth - spiritually and mentally. Use me as a vessel Lord to teach my family of the divine power we are as the body of Christ. In Jesus name I pray, amen."

Fathers [and mothers], do not embitter your children, or they will become discouraged."
-Colossians 3:21 NIV

As mothers, we should feel compelled to lead by example when we are teaching our children how to be pleasing to God. One way to do this is to be mindful and practice living by the fruits of the Spirit:

Love- we should love each other just as Christ Jesus loves us. We should love people where they are, not where we want them to be.

Joy- focus on the goodness of God and find gratitude in every situation, especially the difficult ones.

Peace- through prayer, train yourself to extend grace and forgiveness freely and readily to others. Allow yourself to become a peacemaker, navigating through conflict with active listening and understanding.

Forbearance- do not hold on to your anger and resentments. Instead, find forgiveness and patience for those who need it the most. No one is perfect except the Father and that is a prime example of why you should not expect perfection from others.

Kindness- show compassion, love, and generosity to everyone.

Goodness- seek to actively reflect God's goodness through compassion and kindness. Practicing each of the fruits will allow you to reflect God in this manner.

Faithfulness- read His word daily and maintain your relationship with Him through prayer. Be obedient in all things that you do and keep God at the center of it all.

Gentleness- treat others as you would want to be treated, and do not judge anyone.

Self-control- this one is so easy to lose sight of. How quickly are we to fall into temptation, whether it be on our phones or with the entertainment we allow in our minds? Refrain from temptation and refrain from ever losing control. Diligently remain patient, kind, loving, and compassionate every day.

"Heavenly Father, I come before you today desiring the fruits that you have outlined in your word. By these fruits, I can lead my daughters to exemplify you in all things. Please give me the strength to love everyone the same way you love them. Help me to find joy, especially through the difficult experiences I go through daily - help me to consider it joyous to go through these trying moments. Allow me to have peace and to be at peace, fully trusting you and confident that you are by my side to help me through the storm. God, I now ask you for the fruit of forbearance and the ability to let go of all my anger and resentments. I know this anger only poisons me and I no longer want this. Through my faithfulness, please God, give me kindness, goodness, and gentleness throughout all my daily interactions. Please give me the self-control to embody these fruits today, tomorrow, and the days to come. Through these trials God, let me trust you. Let me know you. Through you, let me show my children the way to be faithful to you through these acts. Soften their hearts and allow them to only know the fruits of the spirit Father God. Help me guide their childhood to create strong adults who don't struggle with these like I do. I ask for your forgiveness and grace as I strive to do better. In Jesus' name I pray, amen."

"But the fruit of the Spirit is love, joy, peace, forbearance, kindness, goodness, faithfulness, gentleness and self-control. Against such things there is no law." **-Galatians 5:22-23 NIV**

Our bodies are temples, filled with the holy spirit and we should honor ourselves in the highest manner. It is so easy to be led into temptation and put things of this world into our temples, not cautious of the consequences. It's more than just respecting ourselves; it's the media we consume, the substances we ingest, and the influences we choose to be around. God doesn't want us to contaminate his space. Every day we should strive to do better and pray to God, the Father, to help us clean our bodies and our minds.

As we raise our children, it is important to show them what is fruitful to place in our temples. It's so easy to find ourselves not paying attention to the things of this world that are not good for our children. We should limit their time on the internet and playing video games. We should encourage them to be well-rested, eat healthy, and read the Word of God daily.

"Heavenly Father, I come to you today to ask you to cleanse my body and the bodies of my children. I ask that you help them to respect their bodies the same way they would respect a temple of God. Please give me the knowledge to know what is pleasing to you so I may pass down that knowledge to them as they grow into adults who can manage their own body. In a world where we so freely give ourselves to each other, I beg you to place it on the hearts and minds of my children to be mindful of the value that they carry as children of God. I ask you these things in Jesus' name, amen."

"Do you not know that your bodies are temples of the Holy Spirit, who is in you, whom you have received from God? You are not your own; you were bought at a price. Therefore, honor God with your bodies. " **-1 Corinthians 6:19-20 NIV**

As a child, I was hurt so deeply by men that I have grown up to have a fear and distrust for any man who is not family. From this pain and trauma, I allowed myself to be put in relationships that were not biblical, desperate for a protector, and I often wondered why I continued to be abused. On my walk in faith now, I see that God clearly outlines the expectations for a man as it pertains to his wife, and in this moment, through scripture, I have the ability to teach my daughters what the standard should be for the men they choose to marry. See, God has given me the great task of raising two beautiful daughters, but He also did this knowing that I fear for their safety and well-being in a world lacking faith. But God has also given me a man who exemplifies the very definition of a husband, one who loves me, just as Christ loved the church. A man who loves me as he loves himself. Through this biblical bond, the marriage that we share, we have the ability to show our daughters firsthand what the expectations should be for the men who court them one day. Together, we can protect them from the world and shield their childhoods so that they grow up without the same abuse I endured. For this, I am abundantly grateful.

"Heavenly Father, thank you for the testimony you have given me and the chance to relive my childhood through my daughters. As I guide them through life, God, I thank you for giving me a husband who lives up to the standards of a Godly man as you clearly defined in the scriptures. In this way, I ask that you create men who will cross paths with my daughters, who will love them as he loves himself. A man who will treat them the way he would treat a church. Allow my daughters to experience this love humbly and without taking it for granted, instead respecting the relationship and the husbands that they will have. In Jesus' name I pray, amen."

"Husbands, love your wives, just as Christ loved the church and gave himself up for her to make her holy, cleansing her by the washing with water through the word, and to present her to himself as a radiant church, without stain or wrinkle or any other blemish, but holy and blameless. In this same way, husbands ought to love their wives as their own bodies. He who loves his wife loves himself." **-Ephesians 5:25-28 NIV**

As we live here on earth, we are constantly surrounded by people. It is inevitable that someone isn't going to like us. In fact, some people may even hate us. The feelings may be mutual, or we may have our own person we just do not like.

Raising children is hard, but raising girls is difficult when you're trying to teach them to live as Jesus did. He tells us to love our enemies and to do good to them, but we can all agree that that is rarely an easy task to do. In our moments of pain, annoyance, frustration, and anger, it's far easier to wish bad on those who have wronged us. It takes a spiritually mature person to find forgiveness and then take it a step further to find love for their enemies. As mothers, we should lead by example every single day so that our children can mimic us, especially in our moments of weakness. We should be able to show our children how to pause and pray for God to give us the strength to pray for our enemies and to give them anything with no expectation of reciprocation. Because when you love your enemies, God rewards you greatly, and your children will be children of the Most High.

"Heavenly Father, I thank you for the people you have placed in my path who have wronged me and hurt me so deeply. This test of faithfulness and obedience is one that I struggle with, but I'm asking you today, Lord, to take that struggle away from me. Let me lead my children by example by loving my enemies, doing good for those who hate me, and blessing those who curse me. Please give me the guidance to teach these principles of Jesus to my children, now while they are children, so that they may become adults who are free from resentments. Because to love your enemy is to be free from the chains of resentment and anger, and to be free is how I pray my children will live. In Jesus' name I pray, amen."

"But to you who are listening I say: Love your enemies, do good to those who hate you, [28] bless those who curse you, pray for those who mistreat you." -**Luke 6:27-28 NIV**

ASHLEY KIDWELL

Contributing Author

Hi, I'm Ashley Kidwell. I was born and raised in Tucson, Arizona, and my journey has been anything but easy — but it is my story and I'm proud of it. I have a Bachelor's degree in Human Resource Management, and I've always had a passion for people — understanding them, supporting them, helping them grow. But before I could truly help others, I had to go through my own process of healing.

For a while, I struggled with substance use. It was one of the hardest chapters of my life, but it also became one of the most defining. Getting through it taught me strength I didn't know I had. It reminded me of what really matters: faith, family, honesty, grace, and the power of starting over.

Today, I'm a wife and a mom of two amazing kids. They are my everything and my why. Life is far from perfect, but it's real, it's beautiful, and it's mine. I'm still growing, still learning, and still trying to show up as the best version of myself every day.

If there's one thing I've learned, it's this: you're never too far gone, never too broken, and never too late to become who you're meant to be.

Apostle
Beverly
Medley

PRAYERS FROM BEVERLY'S HEART

One of the most powerful tools we have today is prayer. Prayer is a form of communication with GOD, our HEAVENLY FATHER, and only produces results when we talk to and listen to HIM. Prayer does not begin for a mother at motherhood, nor does it start for a child at the time of conception. Prayer does not begin for your child(ren) when you learn of the conception. Instead, prayer starts in the womb of the spirit. Prayer should be a proactive approach to life, not a reactive one.

The womb of the spirit is a concept in spirituality that refers to a center of consciousness and creativity.

It serves as a space for nurturing, transformation, and healing.

The womb of the spirit serves as a center of consciousness that functions on various spiritual levels.

It is a space of envelopment, nurturing hold, and generative vitality. It is a place where productivity is conceived.

The womb of the spirit is a place of healing and liberation that can transcend categorical identifications.

God created the woman from the womb of the man, for the man. And wired her with the ability and the capacity to incubate, give birth, nurture, and train up a child.

God is all-powerful and all-wise. You created his inmost being and knitted him together in my womb. Psalm 139:13-16 NIV

LET'S PRAY...

Read and meditate on the prayer below. Then, use the space provided to write your own prayer.

Gracious and all-wise God, I humbly come before You in the name of Jesus Christ of Nazareth. I give You praise, glory, and honor. You are our Majesty. I magnify You and glorify You. I praise You for your marvelous works and your mighty acts. God, you created the woman from the womb of the man, for the man. And wired her with the ability and the capacity to incubate, give birth, nurture, and train up a child. God, You created my inmost being; You knit me together in my mother's womb. Father, I will praise You, for I am fearfully and wonderfully made; marvelous are Thy works, and that my soul knows right well. Your hands crafted me with great respect, honor, and reverence, which sets me apart from others. Thank YOU for making me your masterpiece, in JESUS' name, amen.

LET'S PRAY...

Read and meditate on the prayer below. Then, use the space provided to write your own prayer.

Father, I am grateful for the miracle of childbirth and the gift of motherhood, which will forever leave me in awe of YOU. Your word declares that a woman, when she is in labor, has sorrow because her hour has come; but as soon as she has given birth to the child, she no longer remembers the anguish, for joy that a human being has been born into the world." Father, thank you for the ability to be fruitful and multiply. I am grateful for your Holy Ghost, who leads and guides us into motherhood. Father, thank You that I will be saved in childbearing as I continue in faith, love, and holiness, with self-control. Father, I am grateful for the gift called life, in JESUS' name. Amen.

LET'S PRAY...

Read and meditate on the prayer below. Then, use the space provided to write your own prayer.

God has already predetermined life's events and knows what will be before we ask. Jeremiah 1:5 states, "Before I formed you in the womb I knew you, before you were born, I set you apart; I appointed you as a prophet to the nations."

Father, like Jeremiah, you knew my child and set him apart before he was formed in the womb. You prepared him for a specific purpose and work. Your thoughts were of peace, not evil, to give him an expected end. God, I know You have a specific purpose and plan for his life. I pray that he will rise to the occasion and blossom into the mighty man of valor that he is destined to be. I am forever grateful for your love that allowed me to conceive and give birth to a child. Father, as I lift him before you, I am reminded of YOUR word which tells us we must train up a child in the way he should go, and when he is old, he will not depart from it. I pray that he makes You proud as he seeks ye first the kingdom of God and Your righteousness that all things shall be added unto him, in Jesus' name.

LET'S PRAY...

Father, I pray that my child(ren) will choose to dwell in the secret place of the Most High and abide under the shadow of the Almighty. Cause this dwelling to be their resting place. I declare that they shall be delivered from the snare of the fowler and the noisome pestilence. I pray he will recognize that Your truth is his shield and buckler. I pray that his trust shall continuously be in You. He will not be afraid for the terror by night, nor the arrow that flies by day. Nor for the pestilence that walks in darkness; nor for the destruction that wastes at noonday. A thousand shall fall at his side and ten thousand at his right hand, but it shall not come near his dwelling. I declare that no evil shall befall him. No weapon that is formed against him shall prosper, and every tongue that shall rise against him in judgment shall be condemned.

Father, I ask you to protect him in every area of his life. Fill him with wisdom, knowledge, and understanding. Cause him to respond to the things he suffers with obedience to you. I pray that your Holy Ghost will teach him to bridle his tongue and live integrally. I am forever grateful to you for loving us so much that YOU gave YOUR only begotten SON, that we may have life and have it more abundantly. I declare that he shall live in abundance of Your goodness and mercy, in Jesus' name, amen.

LET'S PRAY...

Read and meditate on the prayer below. Then, use the space provided to write your own prayer.

Heavenly FATHER, in the name of JESUS CHRIST of Nazareth, I thank YOU for revealing Yourself to my child(ren). I am grateful that every promise YOU made before the foundations of the world will manifest as the scales are removed from their eyes. FATHER, it is declared that Your Word is a lamp unto our feet and a light unto our path. YOUR Word also declares that straight is the gate and narrow is the way. And because YOUR Word is a lamp unto our feet and a light unto our path, I thank YOU that the lamp illuminating the path to the narrow way and righteousness shall be their portion. I am grateful that You are our Shepherd, and we shall not want for anything. I pray that they will receive you as Savior and Lord. I pray that my children will make room for You to Lord over every area of their life. Lord over their thoughts, their gifts and talents, their business, their finances and their ministry. I declare that no good thing shall be withheld from them. I ask that You grant them clarity of thought when making decisions, in the name of JESUS, amen.

_____

_____

_____

_____

_____

_____

_____

_____

LET'S PRAY...

Read and meditate on the prayer below. Then, use the space provided to write your own prayer.

FATHER in the name of JESUS, the author and finisher of our faith, our great rewarder. I thank You that, without fail, new mercies are released every morning. FATHER, Your Word has already been established as the foundation for a well-lived life. According to John 6:35, your word declares that JESUS is the bread of life, he that comes to HIM shall never hunger and he that believes shall never thirst. Therefore, I declare that your Word shall be his daily bread. I pray that he shall hunger and thirst after righteousness and be filled. FATHER cause him to be bold, strong, a generational curse breaker, and a generational blessing maker, in the name of JESUS, amen.

LET'S PRAY...

Read and meditate on the prayer below. Then, use the space provided to write your own prayer.

Father, thank You that every chain will be broken off my child(ren's) mind. I declare that they will be loosed from bondage in the name of JESUS. I ask You to protect and keep them safe from all hurt, harm, and danger. I pray that they shall be laser focused, and discernment is sharpened. I pray that thy rod and thy staff shall comfort them all the days of their lives and they will dwell in Your house forever. I declare that my child(ren) will walk in great wisdom and understanding. I declare that they shall have wisdom beyond their years. I pray that they will have the tongue of the learned, that they should know how to speak a word in season to him who is weary. I declare that they shall be lenders and not the borrowers. I pray that my children will be diligent in business, ministry and life affairs as they put their hands to the plow and never look back. I declare that their eyes will be fixed on You and Your word. I pray that the eyes of their understanding shall be enlightened. I pray that their spiritual sight will cause them to see the enemy afar off. Teach them how to be still and know that You are GOD. Teach my child(ren) Your ways. I declare that they will carry Your spirit and host Your presence, in the name of JESUS, amen.

LET'S PRAY...

Read and meditate on the prayer below. Then, use the space provided to write your own prayer.

Father, as Paul and Silas prayed at midnight and the prison doors opened and the chains were broken, if there would ever be a midnight season in his life cause him to have a Paul and Silas experience. Prove Yourself to him in the name of JESUS. I declare that every imagination and every high thing that exalts itself against the knowledge of GOD will be cast down. Every thought shall be brought into captivity to the obedience of CHRIST. I declare that GOD shall release in abundance, he shall have more than enough, too much. Overflow shall be his portion, in JESUS' name, amen.

LET'S PRAY...

Read and meditate on the prayer below. Then, use the space provided to write your own prayer.

Father in the name of JESUS, I come against every demonic force that is trying to assassinate my child(ren's) character and their ability to take authority in the realm of the spirit. Father, as I continue to stand in the gap, I come against every fiery dart that has been launched by the enemy trying to penetrate secured territory. In the name of JESUS. I take authority over the prince of the power of the air and bind every hindering force sent to delay answers to this prayer. We cast down every sinful deed that has been plaguing their minds, in JESUS' name, amen.

LET'S PRAY...

Read and meditate on the prayer below. Then, use the space provided to write your own prayer.

Father, in the name of JESUS, I pray and confess Your Word over every child, surrounding them with my faith. YOUR Word declares that You perfect those things that concern me. Therefore, I commit and cast the care of my child(ren) on You. I put them in Your hands, and I am persuaded that You can guard and keep that which I have committed to You. FATHER, as I stand in agreement with YOUR Word, I declare that children will begin to obey their parents in the LORD. I pray that they will honor and esteem them highly, that all may be well and they may live long on the earth. Father, I thank You for giving Your angels charge over every child to defend them, You are the glory and the lifter of their heads, in the name of JESUS, amen.

Father, in the name of JESUS, our Supreme Being, the everlasting Father, and eternal GOD, thank YOU for Your supernatural manifestation of YOUR power in my child(ren)'s life. I am grateful for YOUR divine nature. You are omnipotent (all-powerful), omniscient (all-knowing), omnipresent (ever-present). I declare that they will have divine connections and right relationships. Thank YOU for honoring their seeking of divine increase in wisdom, knowledge, and understanding. I pray for divine healing over their minds, bodies, and emotions.

I pray they recognize GOD given territory. Wherever the soles of their feet tread, shall be their portion. I declare they shall walk in GOD-given authority, which grants them the ability to tread upon serpents and scorpions, and nothing shall by any means hurt them, in the name of JESUS. Father, since we wrestle not against flesh and blood but against demonic principalities, demonic powers, rulers of the darkness of this age, and spiritual wickedness in high places, I declare my child(ren) to be fully dressed for the battle. I pray that they will put on the whole armor of GOD, so that they may be able to stand against the wiles of the devil and withstand the evil days. I pray their loins are girded with truth and their hearts shielded with the breastplate of righteousness. Father, lead them to cover their feet with the preparation of the gospel of peace, and above all, I pray they will be protected by the shield of faith that they may be able to quench all the fiery darts of the wicked. I declare that the helmet of salvation and the sword of the Spirit shall be their portion, in JESUS' name.

I come against the spirit of procrastination and declare that it will not overpower their minds. Answered prayers will no longer be hindered, and miracles will not be held up, in the name of JESUS, amen.

BEVERLY MEDLEY

Contributing Author

Beverly is a North Carolina native with a deep love for prayer and intercession. She is an apostle, prophet, teacher, preacher, mentor, counselor, and intercessor. She is also the CEO and founder of Beverly Medley Ministries, No Compromise Movement, Kingdom Etiquette, and I am SHE. Beverly is the mother of one son, Jeremy, and has grandchildren. Driven by her calling and personal experiences, she felt compelled by love to establish Beverly Medley Ministries, which serves all people with purpose, effectiveness, power, and prayer. Later, she founded the No Compromise Movement, Kingdom Etiquette, and I am SHE. Beverly is uniquely gifted and a born-again, Spirit-Filled Woman of God, striving to become more like Christ.

Jessica
Lescano

PRAYERS FROM JESSICA'S HEART

HELLO FELLOW MOTHERS!

My name is Jessica. I was born in Queens NY, raised in Allentown Pennsylvania. I have been married for less than a year to one of my Greatest Gifts, Evangelist Tyeson Douglas. I am a mother of three, Corey, Leevi, and Journey. I have a blended family, Tyeson Jr and Genesis, who are mine through my husband. I also have bonus children that are siblings to my daughter Journey; Jaylanys, Alexia, Francisco III and Sanyiah. They are all my babies, and no one can tell me different. I am the oldest daughter of four girls, so my parenting began before even bringing up my own children. Lastly, I am an aunt (Titi), another amazing gift, my first nephew I call phew'son, Nazyre; Massiah and Siege.

Interesting fact about me, I was saved in September of 2022; some may say I'm a baby in Christ, but I say, I'm no baby in faith. I write spoken word poetry to glorify our heavenly father; to set free the captives, brokenhearted and the lost; with the flowing word. I am not the perfect mother, but I am a dedicated mom and about my father's business. As for me and my house, we will serve the Lord. Jesus is the only way to be set free from the trauma we have endured, the only way to break generational curses, the only way to be sane, in parenting. Continue to seek our Lord, and he will walk with you, in all truth.

We can pray many times over our children, but first we need to be able to accept that we are not their savior, there is only one, Jesus! They will bump their heads, they will make mistakes and fall short, as we all do. As a mother it is so hard to stay focused on who is in control.

We want what is best, we want easy flow, we want routine, and no snippy attitudes, what an imagination I say. When we can humble ourselves and be accountable for our actions, find our identity in Christ, the steps to parenting will unravel. What I will share with you is allow your child/ren to hear you love them more than social media does, on the outside we are able to express this, but are you as a parent able to endure and love unconditionally even when your child is being rebellious. Lead by example. Are you "practicing what you preach" in the home? Parenting is not easy when you're walking out of the order of GOD. Prayer is needed; Prayer is going to get you through. He, GOD, is going to change your babies' hearts as you water them. Stop trying to do it on your own and do it with God. Our children are made in the image of GOD as well, (please remember that) when your frustrations get the best of you.

God bless you Mommy!
-Jessica

I DIDN'T KNOW

First born, thought I knew everything when I had you,
all I knew was how to do what I wanted to,
was young, wanted my own family,
trying to escape childhood trauma, finally live in reality,
with you.
Not knowing that my role as a mother,
wasn't just taking you to appointments, following up after surgeries,
wasn't to yell, when you made mistakes, or to get frustrated,
when the homework assigned you couldn't complete.
It wasn't just to buy you everything,
or to make sure your sneakers were up to date,
it wasn't to show you off on social media
and brag that I am doing my thing.

You grew up with me, and watched me struggle with so many things,
you stood by me, even comforted me along the way.
I was giving you a role, that isn't a child's place,
can't seem to get it out my head that I owe you an apology.
I am sorry I didn't hear you, when you said "I don't know how"
I am sorry I didn't hear you when words didn't flow out,
but your eyes screamed that all you needed was a hug,
to show you now, I am sorry that I didn't know how to be what you
needed me to be,
I didn't know love, unconditionally.
I am sorry that I loved you with expectation, not seeing that,
the watering you needed was not that.
I thank nothing but JESUS for you being who you are to me.

I am sorry that I thought you were better off without me, and sent you off, thinking I couldn't protect you because I was thrown off.

I am sorry that I showed you a wicked lifestyle, but oh how I thank nothing but Jesus, for how you turned out.

I am sorry that I wasn't available mentally,
thought if I fed you, clothed you and took you out,
that everything else would all play out.

I am sorry that I didn't even try to stay in a marriage, pushing my way out from your father.

I wanted things my way and not to be told how,
I am sorry that I wasn't healed.

All I knew was survival, how to do it one way, closed off to the inner healing, and repetitive ways.

I am sorry it took me so long to sit down, to figure out the way, but I vowed that it stops at me.

No more hindering, from a trauma full history,
this generation, will be a healed visionary.

Now I know your safe, I can sleep sound.

When I walk by and you're kneeling, praying for your way,
I can't thank anything but Jesus for showing me how.

Love you Pac!

YOU & I

The Breeze swirling into a sense of relief,
feeling nature through my fingertips, feet hit the sand,
warmed my body, the heat from the bottom of my feet,
sizzled through my veins, gliding towards the water holding onto my
developed stomach,
knowing the world is crashing in, as the waves sounds trinkle within,
knowing the stingrays of pain,
I trapped myself in,
individuals, telling me to let you go,
darkness surrounding,
just me and you aiming to match the speed of the torrent,
you and I, will get through the foggy atmosphere

Not a soul can make a forced action to change my mind,
the enemy was in disguise,
you have been one of my reasons,
to stay alive, ever since, I felt your kick,
you have been a source of strength, encouragement,
even while dealing with trauma and depression,
your light was presented, would see me on the bathroom floor,
wipe my tears so gently, already at the age of three,
no one can tell me that you weren't meant to be here, with me,
decided to keep a lie hidden,
so that humankind wouldn't make you feel unwanted or as hopeless
as I did.

You are a rising star, a resilient child, God saw before me,
I walked into a fire, & played in many schemes,
he was already in there

awaiting me, not on my time, but on his, rescuing us,
we didn't even know who he was, isn't that miraculous,
so watching you grow has been so mysterious,
such a test and after many years,
I finally realized that I was not here to save you even though you
were innocent to all this,
I am not a savior of my own, my duty is to point you in the right
direction, to plant into your soil, focus your eyes on,
not right, but righteous, and let His work guide within,
many disruptions has happened since, the world took you off
course, following friends,
but Prayerfully God snatched you back in

He chose you to be on this earth when I, was told to let it go, run,
I was in so much pain I didn't know how to raise or mother you,
so I just kept giving in, I kept giving you, your wants,
enabling them by remembering the pain,
I first endured when I found out the seed
in me was already planted,
as you get older and I watch you lean on your peers to figure out
this cruel world,
insecurity of myself kicks in, know that I will never give up on you,
I pray each day that the Lord blocks your ear gates,
that you're convicted when you're about to walk into sin,
you're such an inspiring story, the reconciliation between me and
your father is only because of God's glory, as you grow,
I'll continue to water, will continue to pray, that no matter what
your testimony shows the love of God,
because your mom never gave in to the noise of wickedness,
you are meant to live!

Love you Man!

IT'S ME, NOT YOU

Gentle wind, pleasing white clouds, blue sky,
standing boldly behind, moving profoundly,
when your eyes look into mine, I would see my reflection,
heart glimmered, your presence was so peaceful,
didn't think I can nurture you, so fear became the focus,
instead of loving on you,
and allowing you to walk into your character,
my past trauma, started being yours,
yells would roar when I was disappointed in a minor error,
because you haven't matured, didn't want you to witness,
things I experienced, how can I protect someone so innocent,
without wounding, overloading you into the same pattern,
as I walked in, don't know what soft girl era is,
I'm a boy mom, God, you just rooted pain,
inadequate of raising such a graceful girl, couldn't see the lesson
then, or the restraints being broken, until I gained understanding of,
everything being done, for a purpose, beautiful divine girl, planted a
seed in the soil, you were created with, irrigating daily, pouring into
you, your child-like mind spraying into mommy, now knowing you
are molded into an individual being, identity isn't in me, uniquely
made, given thought to, never want you to think that you're in
competition with another, or even fighting a battle, that isn't yours in
the first place, complaints settled, for apprehension, love guided,
which seemed so simple, took me out the way and see you through
the lens of the creator, you are the queen who helped me see, that
the only way to raise you, guide you, love you, is to, is to bow the
knee. I thank God for a renewal in human form, I will hold your hand
through every storm, until we meet the gentle wind, pleasing white
clouds and blue sky standing bold behind.

Love you Mama

IT'S ME, NOT YOU

Gentle wind, pleasing white clouds, blue sky, standing boldly behind, moving profoundly, when your eyes look into mine, I would see my reflection, heart glimmered, your presence was so peaceful, didn't think I can nurture you, so fear became the focus, instead of loving on you, and allowing you to walk into your character, my past trauma, started being yours, yells would roar when I was disappointed in a minor error, because you haven't matured, didn't want you to witness, things I experienced, how can I protect someone so innocent, without wounding, overloading you into the same pattern, as I walked in, don't know what soft girl era is, I'm a boy mom, God, you just rooted pain, inadequate of raising such a graceful girl, couldn't see the lesson then, or the restraints being broken, until I gained understanding of, everything being done, for a purpose, beautiful divine girl, planted a seed in the soil, you were created with, irrigating daily, pouring into you, your child-like mind spraying into mommy, now knowing you are molded into an individual being, identity isn't in me, uniquely made, given thought to, never want you to think that you're in competition with another, or even fighting a battle, that isn't yours in the first place, complaints settled, for apprehension, love guided, which seemed so simple, took me out the way and see you through the lens of the creator, you are the queen who helped me see, that the only way to raise you, guide you, love you, is to, is to bow the knee. I thank God for a renewal in human form, I will hold your hand through every storm, until we meet the gentle wind, pleasing white clouds and blue sky standing bold behind.

Love you Mama

MOMMY'S PRAYER

Our father who are in heaven Hallowed be thy name
thy Kingdom come thy will be done,
on earth as it is in heaven give us this day Our Daily Bread,
Father please guide my children, their hearts,
block their ear gates from the sinful fantasies,
allow them to know who you are, as I stand in the doorway,
of the tragedies from our past, in your name fighting the attacks,
opening doors knowingly, unknowingly,
to the darkness that can imitate what you're trying to fulfill,
allow the imitations to decrease in their concept,
I cast it down in the name of Jesus, father God,
you are all knowing, you are powerful, I pray for my children,
that each and every one of them find their identity
only through you, and not try to be pleasing to unsettle minds,
Father God, I thank you in advance for them
coming to everlasting life, meeting me, greeting me there,
to hold my hand for eternity, not just worried about the sacrifices
that have been made on a solid land,

Jesus I call out to you that your precious blood would be over my
children, their children, and their children's children,
from this day forward, I stand at the access point
on behalf of the Son of Mans Kingdom,
Father God, I rebuke the attempts of the enemy that tries,
tries to bring insecurity because they don't have something,
that someone else has, Father God I reprove anything that's trying
to come against them to make them feel unworthy

I ask that you hold them in your precious right hand,
continue to show them the way,
not by my eagerness to have them know you,
but by the eagerness of Your will to be done,
here on Earth as it is in Heaven,
Father God, forgive us for our trespasses,
as we forgive them that trespass against us,
let it be known, no matter who has hurt us,
we're able to forgive, forgiving for you and not unto them,
we're forgiving to be released from captivity,
not for our friends, or ideologies,
release us from the spiritual realm that wants to keep us stagnant,
stored in a cage,
Jesus, Father God, I hand over this battle back to you,
it never belonged to me, it's too heavy to try to eliminate,
lead us not into temptation but deliver us from evil,
all the petty thoughts and bitterness that we hold on to,
I cast down in the name of Jesus,
the things that we think were supposed to feel and say,
because they show unkind ways,
allow our daughters and our sons to bear the image of Christ,
not what they have been exposed to through social media,
and friends that don't seek Christ,
for is thy Kingdom the power and the glory
forever and ever, nobody can take over what You've already
spoken, can't reiterate a word that you have given,
our hearts are the soil, as parents directed to plant the seed in,
guide us to water our children, with the love that you have for us,
that this world seems not to believe in,
the love that we have for you will not go in vain,
the knee that we bow will not go untamed,
breaking generational curses,

it stopped at me, all the past is already history,
told us do not look back, you are there behind,
see before and stand beside, grieved when we cry,
you are the one that we need to lean into,
the one that we need to be begging and pleading,
not asking our children why, why are they like this,
we know that there are also prone to the attack,
these things are generational, not shown clearly,
seen in part, in this world, that's tearing us apart,
you did not cause division between us,
we're allowing captivity and deceitfulness to lead us into remission,

Father God as I'm praying out to You,
I ask that You release the mothers' minds back into your hands,
show us that we can go back to that childlike mind,
crawl up into a fetus, also your children,
just need your word to empower, get us through,
enable us to armor up starting with the shoes,
not the thought our immediate response triggers,
give us your understanding, give us your wisdom, Yes!

God give us the wisdom, so that we don't walk into a battlefield,
let us hand the war back over, you gave us the victory,
our endurance created character,
our strength only came from you,
you isolated us in those moments so that we can only seek you,
not what others do, we won't be displaced, you asked us to
Steward over your children, we are all made of the image of you,
even our children, which we need to be reminded,

it isn't our way, I give you thanks, I give you honor,
I give you all the glory, for the breakthroughs and reoccurring
journeys, that you allow to take place,
until we walk into paradise,
God we are here to be pleasing to you,
Allow our parenting to bare up the cross,
even midday when we feel like we're falling apart,
Thank you, Father, thank you for the authority in Jesus Christ,
Thank you for your unconditional love and sacrifice.
In Jesus' name we pray, amen.

JESS LESCANO

Contributing Author

My name is Jessica. I was born in Queens NY, raised in Allentown Pennsylvania. I have been married for less than a year to one of my Greatest Gifts, Evangelist Tyeson Douglas. I am a mother of three, Corey, Leevi, and Journey. I have a blended family, Tyeson Jr and Genesis, who are mine through my husband. I also have bonus children that are siblings to my daughter Journey; Jaylanys, Alexia, Francisco III and Sanyiah. They are all my babies, and no one can tell me different. I am the oldest daughter of four girls, so my parenting began before even bringing up my own children. Lastly, I am an aunt (Titi), another amazing gift, my first nephew I call phew'son, Nazyre; Massiah and Siege.

Interesting fact about me, I was saved in September of 2022; some may say I'm a baby in Christ, but I say, I'm no baby in faith. I write spoken word poetry to glorify our heavenly father; to set free the captives, brokenhearted and the lost; with the flowing word. I am not the perfect mother, but I am a dedicated mom and about my father's business. As for me and my house, we will serve the Lord.

Jesus is the only way to be set free from the trauma we have endured, the only way to break generational curses, the only way to be sane, in parenting. Continue to seek our Lord, and he will walk with you, in all truth.

Samantha
NaCole

PRAYERS FROM SAMANTHA'S HEART

Read and meditate on the prayer below, then use the space provided to write your own prayer.

My God in Heaven,

Thank you for your new grace and new mercy today. I thank you for breathing your breath into my children's lungs. I know you've equipped me with all the tools I need to be their Mother. God, whatever I can't do, I know you can. Protect them in their goings and comings. Take control of their mind. Let Your voice and Your voice only be heard. When their hearts are broken, and they can't understand why, allow them to rest in Your arms, as-well-as hear Your voice. I pray a hedge of protection all around them daily, in Jesus' name, amen.

Read and meditate on the prayer below, then use the space provided to write your own prayer.

My God in Heaven,

Our children need you more and more as we live in this crazy world. The enemy wants them to think they are not who You purposely created them to be, but we rebuke that evil spirit and cast it back to the pits of hell where it belongs in the name of Jesus. I thank you for giving me a tongue that has the power of authority to speak prosperity, healing, and deliverance over my children. We will never settle for less than when we serve a BIG GOD! In Jesus' name I pray, amen.

Read and meditate on the prayer below, then use the space provided to write your own prayer.

My God in Heaven,

I come to You as humble as I know how to first of all thank You for this day. Lord, as my adult children seek to find their way down here, lead them to the path of righteousness. In their times of trouble, confusion, sadness, or grieve I pray You are the one they run to wholeheartedly. If they ever lose their way, leave the 99 to go and get my child, your precious heir. When they forget, remind them of who You are and who they are. You've loaned them to us for a little while, so while they're here, I dedicate them back to You because You are the only One who can! In Jesus' name I pray, amen.

A Prayer for my Son Who Has Been Diagnosed with Autism

My God in Heaven,

I am forever grateful to you for blessing me to be the earthly Mother to your heir. I don't know what I've done to deserve such a sweet soul, but I'm so grateful. I know you have already placed it in me to be all that he needs me to be. I ask that you teach me. As his voice for a short while, give me the wisdom to speak his language. Help us to understand each other. When he's hurting or isn't feeling too well, please, God heal him. Please let him know I love him, and I'm right here to comfort him. Bless me with the knowledge to share with others so that they can understand why he's not responding to them. I can't do but so much, but my God, my God, you can. Protect him, especially when I'm not around him. I plead the blood of Jesus over him right now in Jesus' name. Touch his heart and let him know I love him and he's not alone. You spoke a special word to me over his life, and I trust and believe you for it daily. To witness your glory, I thank you! In Jesus' name I pray, amen.

A Prayer for my Daughter Who Has an Absent Father

My God in Heaven,

The choices I've made not only affected me but also my children. I ask for forgiveness. Please mend my daughter's broken heart from the absence of her father. She doesn't understand why. As she prays to You, speak to her. When she secretly cries, hold her in Your arms. Let her feel Your peace and Your love. I know that besides my choices, You still have a special plan for her life. Give her the vision to her whys. Give her a song of praise unto Your name for making her beauty from ashes. In Jesus' name, amen.

If you have a child with an absent earthly father, write a prayer for your child below.

A Prayer for my Adult Chid(ren)

My God in Heaven,

As my adult children step out into this world to find their way, their purpose, I'm asking that You guide them. Don't ever let them get so far gone that they can't find their way to You. There are so many lessons to learn, levels to reach, and different seasons they will go through. Let them know they are not alone. This path is given to them with purpose. To make and mold them to be Your disciples. Pour wisdom into them daily. I pray they'll always count it, JOY. In Jesus' name I pray, amen.

Write a prayer for your child(ren) below.

Read and meditate on the prayer below, then use the space provided to write your own prayer.

My God in Heaven,

Depression and suicide are not options for my children. I need Your spirit to pour deep within them. When they can't fight the fight, my God, stand in boldly on their behalf. Just like the dream You gave me where You stood in front of me as the devil tried to get to me. I didn't worry, and I didn't fear because I knew who You were. Every time my children forget, Lord, remind them of who You have created them to be. In Jesus' name, remind them they are loved. Remind them they are needed. Remind them they have purpose. In Jesus' name I pray, amen.

SAMANTHA NACOLE

Contributing Author

Hi, my name is Samantha NaCole. I am a woman after God's own heart. I was born in Shallotte, NC, and raised in Ash, NC. I have 4 wonderful blessings who call me Mom. I am a Cosmetologist who specializes in braids of different sorts. I serve on the media team at church, which I love. In my free time, I enjoy spending it with children and writing. One of God's gifts to me is the use of my hands.

*Yvonne
Salsbury*

PRAYERS FROM YVONNE'S HEART

Prayer: Lord please help me to care for their souls and their spirits as much as I care for their physical needs.

How many times to do you find yourself providing meals for your children? Morning, noon and night. Snacks, special occasions. It feels endless at times, yet we would never consider not feeding our children. Sometimes we feed them nutritional food that really nourishes their bodies. Other times, we feed them fast, quick and easy meals just to give them something. Sometimes we have our go to standards. Chicken nuggets and mac & cheese! Sometimes, we take time to plan out meals that will be satisfying and filling. All of these have their place and meet the physical needs of our children.
What would it look like if we had the same sense of responsibility to feed their spiritual needs? Jesus says that he is the bread of life. (John 6:35) Our children need the one who can truly satisfy their souls. The one who can give them eternal life. The scriptures are clear that Jesus is the one who provides what matters most for our children. Our plea as parents is to ask the Lord to please help us feed our children the word of God on a consistent, daily basis.

Consider a 15 to 20 minute intentional, planned bible study with you child as the equivalent of the planned, nutritional meal. Find something on their level and plan ahead to make it a priority. It doesn't have to be a long process, just like a good meal. It is not the entire day, just a small portion of time; however, it is meaningful and can be greatly anticipated. Consider fast food to be taking advantage of time in the car, after school, or before bed to check in with them to see how their day went and help them see how God may have been at work in their day or how they might be able to navigate difficult situations with peers using biblical principles.

These are the unplanned moments that allow opportunities to help them apply the things they are learning during bible studies, etc. Snacks are those fun moments that we can give praise that thanksgiving for how we are seeing God work in our lives and when he answers prayers. It's really a morning, noon, and night focus on pointing them to the one who created them for His glory. If this feels like it is overwhelming, don't try to do it all at once. Pick one place to start and then add on. But remember, we the Holy Spirt to lead and teach us. As the Spirit gives us wisdom, we will be able to do it. He is our comforter and will strengthen us to do what we are called to do. Jesus says he will never leave us or forsake us, so we can do this. (Matt 28:20)

"But he answered, "It is written, "Man shall not live by bread alone, but by every word that comes from mouth of God." **Matthew 4:4**

Prayer: Lord, please help me to fear you and to teach my children to do the same.

What does it mean to fear the Lord? When we think of fear, it brings up all kinds of emotions depending on the experience of the person. What they have experienced personally and through observation. If we look at humanity and society, we have ample opportunity to see the horror of what man does to each other and fear is a part of our existence, yet scripture teaches us to not fear man, but fear God. The worse thing man can do to us is to kill the body, yet the God of creation can not only kill the body but can also condemn the soul. (Matt 10:28). Yet, we spend our time teaching them about stranger/danger, watch your surroundings, and don't take anything not given to you by a parent or doctor. All very important life lessons, yet the critical truth of fearing God is something we shy away from. We want our children to run to God, to love God and to trust in him for their salvation, and yet we do not teach them that He is a just God and requires obedience. So why is this critical truth so important for our children to learn? The answer is found in the scriptures. "To fear the Lord is the beginning of all wisdom." (Prov 9:10)

Consider Proverbs 1: 20-33. It outlines the real danger of ignoring wisdom. It says that in the day of our trouble, we will call out but we will not receive any help. Psalms 33 also says that the eye of the Lord is on those who fear him, that He may deliver their soul from death and keep them alive in famine. (ESV)

As we think through these implications, we can start with the basics. Let's just look at one of the commandments. "Do not bear false witness" (Exodus 20:16). We would say, "do not lie". How wise is it for a child/person to lie when confronted with a situation?

As parents, don't we say, "If you lie to me about this, it will be so much worse!". We fundamentally know that to lie leads to bigger consequences and often bigger problems. Yet, do we view this as the commandment that it is? Do we fear the God who commanded, "Do not bear false witness?" If not, why not? This same God says you will give an account for every idle word you speak. (Matthew 12:36) Is that a wise course of action? I think we could all agree that it is not.

Our goal as parents is to set our children up for success in life. To see them experience all the good things life can bring, so when wisdom is used this can be a reality. Their family relationships can be dynamic. Their work can be fulfilling. Their relationship with their creator can be deeper and more meaningful as they grow in His grace and wisdom is gained.

We are to train our children in the way they should go, so that when they are old, they do not depart from it. (Prov 22:6) So in that training, we need to train them to fear God. What better gift could we give them than to understand they should obey the one who made them. Therefore, we cry out to God and ask Him to help us first fear Him properly and then help us to teach our children to do the same. We do this by studying the scriptures and learning what it means to fear the Lord. This is not something that a quick devotional can provide. This is something that takes time to seek out. One habit I have when trying to understand or gain knowledge in a particular area is to have a notebook and jot down every time I see a reference to that topic. I can then see the context that it was written in and I pray and ask the Holy Spirit to guide my understanding of the scriptures as I am reading. There are no shortcuts to parenting. There are no quick fixes, but there is the Word of God that brings wisdom.

"Today I set before you life and death, a blessing and a curse. Choose life!" -**Deuteronomy 30:19**

Prayer: Father, please help me to teach my children to be doers of the word and not hearers only.

There seems to be a sect of Christianity that would try to have us believe that God will tolerate our fleshly walk. That He loves us so much that he will basically put up with our bad behavior. While there is certainly an element of truth to this, that is how the enemy works. Just enough truth to make it believable, yet it is deception.

Jesus says that if you keep his commandments, that is how you demonstrate that you love him (John 14:15,21) The expectation from the Father is that we walk in obedience. Obedience to what? His word. This is a vital truth for us and for our children. To only read the word and never apply it to our lives, is to miss the whole point.

The desire and work of the Holy Spirit is to conform us into the image of Christ. Though we will all agree that it will not fully happen until we are glorified with him, we are on the journey of sanctification while we are on this earth. The sanctification process is walking in the light. The word of God. Walking indicates action. It is not a passive process. So, if we are to teach our children how they should live, it starts with reading God's word and then doing it.

The scriptures say don't be a hearer only. In the time the scriptures were written, they did not have the printed word as we do today. There were very few copies, and they were given to the community ministers. The custom of the day was to meet, and someone would read the scriptures. Thus, they would hear the word of God. The apostle James is instructing that we should not just read or hear the word, but to take that and do what it says. We can hear a good message straight from the word of God through our pastors or good bible teachers and think, "that was awesome", but the real value, and frankly the expectation, is that it would be put into practice.

"Your word is a lamp to my feel and a light to my path." -**Psalm 119:105**

"But be doers of the word, and not hearers only, deceiving yourselves." -**James 1:22**

When that happens, the Lord is glorified. This is the spiritual discipline our children need. They need to be taught to obey the scriptures. When they read the word or hear the word, they should be thinking, "now how do I apply this in my life?"

Let's look at that in a real-world example. "Children obey your parents in the Lord, for this is right. Honor your father and mother, that it may go well with you and that you may live long in the Lord". (Eph 6:1-2) The practical aspect is that by obeying their parents, things go well for them. Isn't it so much easier for the entire family when children do as they are instructed. They brush their teeth, clean their rooms, and pick up after themselves! Wow, what joy and peace that brings!!! Instead, when they chose not to obey, there are consequences. Electronics are taken away, play time is limited or they are spending all day on a beautiful Saturday cleaning up their mess. These are small issues, but they lead to bigger and more significant life crises if they do not learn to walk in obedience to the word. The extreme might be that they look at scripture and see that it says, "Do not commit adultery", yet they are deceived into thinking that, "God loves me and understands. He wants me to be happy". No, he wants you to obey his word because that is where true happiness comes. Knowing you are right with your creator is a true source of joy and peace.

So back to the beginning, Lord please help us to look at your word with hearts full of obedience that we would do what it says for us to do, knowing that you have put your Holy Spirit in us to enable us to do what you have spoken in your word. Then Father, help us to teach our children to do the same. To look to your word for truth, not be deceived by false teaching, and walking in obedience in all areas of their lives. In Jesus name, amen.

"If we say that we have fellowship with him while we walk in darkness, we lie and do not practice the truth." **-1 John 1:6-9**

YVONNE SALSBURY

Contributing Author

I married to my husband Travis of 24 years and we have two children. Caleb who is 14 and Lizzy who is 7. The Lord blessed through the adoption process and each of the children were 2 years old when they joined the family. I come from a family of 5 children and was not raised in church. I was saved at 10 years of age attending Vacation Bible School with a neighbor. My parents divorced when I was 7 and I was raised in a disfunctional family; however, I've learned that the far majority of us come from less than ideal backgrounds. This just shows the grace of our Lord.

I am a native of Louisiana and have lived in South Carolina for the past 14 years. I currently live in Myrtle Beach where we attended Calvary Bible Church. We love our church family.

I am also a small business owner with 5 employees. Things are always busy in my world. I enjoy reading and going to the beach in my spare time.

PRAYERS FROM YOUR HEART

A MOTHER'S PRAYER...

Date_____

_____

_____

_____

_____

_____

_____

_____

_____

_____

_____

_____

_____

_____

_____

_____

_____

_____

_____

_____

_____

_____

A MOTHER'S PRAYER...

Date_____

A MOTHER'S PRAYER...

Date_____

_____
_____
_____
_____
_____
_____
_____
_____
_____
_____
_____
_____
_____
_____
_____
_____
_____
_____
_____
_____
_____
_____
_____
_____
_____
_____
_____
_____
_____

A MOTHER'S PRAYER...

Date_____

A MOTHER'S PRAYER...

Date_____

A MOTHER'S PRAYER...

Date_____

_____

_____

_____

_____

_____

_____

_____

_____

_____

_____

_____

_____

_____

_____

_____

_____

_____

_____

_____

_____

A MOTHER'S PRAYER...

Date_____

_____

_____

_____

_____

_____

_____

_____

_____

_____

_____

_____

_____

_____

_____

_____

_____

_____

_____

_____

_____

_____

_____

_____

A MOTHER'S PRAYER...

Date_____

_____
_____
_____
_____
_____
_____
_____
_____
_____
_____
_____
_____
_____
_____
_____
_____
_____
_____
_____
_____
_____
_____
_____

A MOTHER'S PRAYER...

Date_____

_____
_____
_____
_____
_____
_____
_____
_____
_____
_____
_____
_____
_____
_____
_____
_____
_____
_____
_____
_____
_____
_____
_____
_____
_____
_____
_____
_____
_____

A MOTHER'S PRAYER...

Date_____

_____

_____

_____

_____

_____

_____

_____

_____

_____

_____

_____

_____

_____

_____

_____

_____

_____

_____

_____

_____

_____

A MOTHER'S PRAYER...

Date_____

_____

_____

_____

_____

_____

_____

_____

_____

_____

_____

_____

_____

_____

_____

_____

_____

_____

_____

_____

_____

_____

_____

_____

_____

_____

A MOTHER'S PRAYER...

Date_____

A MOTHER'S PRAYER...

Date_____

_____
_____
_____
_____
_____
_____
_____
_____
_____
_____
_____
_____
_____
_____
_____
_____
_____
_____
_____
_____

A MOTHER'S PRAYER...

Date_____

A MOTHER'S PRAYER...

Date_____

A MOTHER'S PRAYER...

Date_____

A MOTHER'S PRAYER...

Date_____

_____

_____

_____

_____

_____

_____

_____

_____

_____

_____

_____

_____

_____

_____

_____

_____

_____

_____

_____

_____

_____

_____

_____

_____

A MOTHER'S PRAYER...

Date_____

A MOTHER'S PRAYER...

Date_____

www.ingramcontent.com/pod-product-compliance
Lightning Source LLC
Chambersburg PA
CBHW051227120626
46547CB00013B/1543